ENTERTAINING
IN THE
French Style

Eileen W. Johnson
Photographs by Brie Williams

GIBBS SMITH
TO ENRICH AND INSPIRE HUMANKIND

To Vanessa Brett, my daughter, who taught me
the true meaning of love

First Edition
14 13 12 11 10   5 4 3 2 1

Text © 2010 Eileen W. Johnson
Photographs © 2010 Brie Williams

Published by
Gibbs Smith
P.O. Box 667
Layton, Utah 84041

1.800.835.4993 orders
www.gibbs-smith.com

Designed by Debra McQuiston
Printed and bound in Hong Kong
Gibbs Smith books are printed on paper produced from sustainable PEFC-certified forest/controlled
wood source. Learn more at: www.pefc.org

Library of Congress Cataloging-in-Publication Data

Johnson, Eileen W.
  Entertaining in the French style / Eileen Johnson ; photographs by Brie Williams. — 1st ed.
    p. cm.
  ISBN-13: 978-1-4236-0575-1
  ISBN-10: 1-4236-0575-6
  1. Entertaining—France. 2. Cookery, French. 3. France—Social life and customs. I. Title.
  TX731.J657 2010
  641.5944—dc22
                    2010012659

Contents

Introduction

IN A RECENT INTERVIEW with the former poet laureate Charles Simic, the *New York Times* asked him how he felt about all the nonfiction books recently published on happiness. The writer posed the question, "What advice would you give to people who are looking to be happy?" His answer, "For starters, learn to cook." I would add to that "set a table and entertain friends."

Setting a beautiful table, whether it be informal, formal, country-like, or citified is probably the most joyful part of entertaining. And nowhere in the world has the art of the table been more refined than in France. From the most humble restaurant that serves fish with a proper fish fork and knife to the most exalted meal at the Elysee Palace, the French attention to detail is shown in its glory while serving food.

Setting a beautiful table is the most joyful part of entertaining. And nowhere has the art of the table been more refined than in France.

It has been said that people in France tend not to invite outsiders into their homes, that much entertaining is done in restaurants. Perhaps this is true in Paris where many live in small apartments and it is easier to meet friends at the local café or bistro. But I have found that entertaining at home is still very much a part of life in contemporary France.

One of the great pleasures of my life was putting together this book. Essentially *Entertaining in the French Style* is about sharing love—the love of the land, the love of food being well prepared, the love of home and hearth. I was extremely lucky to be welcomed into so many homes that were abundant in warmth, creativity, and generosity of spirit.

France is a country of many different regions. This book is but a slice of the life that is France today.

Entertaining in the French Style is all about the food. It starts with the land, so rich and fertile, and shows how varied the produce we eat is, depending on where it is grown. It is about the farmers, the butchers, the cheesemakers, and the vast number of artisans who help to bring the food to the table. It is about the craftsmen who create dishes made from techniques that are the same as they were in the eighteenth century. It is about the chefs who prepare the food, the vintners who bottle the wine, but mostly about the many people who take the time and the effort to enjoy all the pleasures of the table with friends and family. Informally or formally—at lunch, at tea, at breakfast, and at dinner—this book is all about entertaining inspired by all things French.

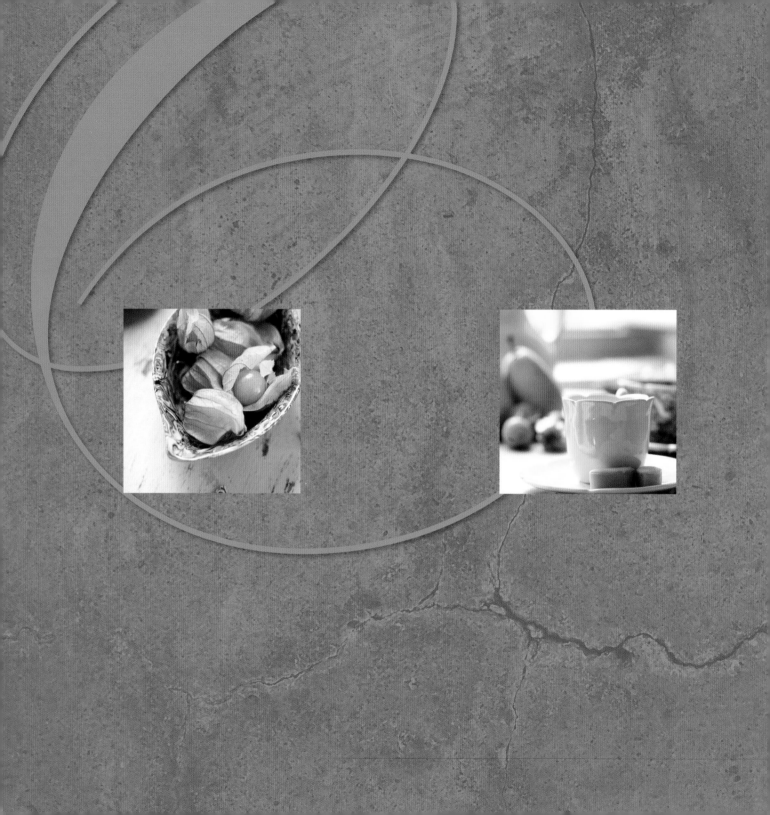

In the Medieval Town of Saignon

In the Medieval Town of Saignon

Breakfast in Bed

A MYSTICAL SHROUD surrounds the small village of Saignon, which is perched overlooking the Luberon Mountains. It has an otherworldly quality to its streets that one might easily define as spiritual. Since the Middle Ages, the twelfth-century church there, known as Saint Mary of Saignon, was a stopping point for religious pilgrims who were traveling to Rome. One can almost hear the footsteps of the devout in the town square with its fountain gently flowing, uninterrupted by the sound of passing automobiles. This town is relatively untouched by the large number of tourists following in the footsteps of Peter Mayle's Provence. Tiny, with just over nine hundred inhabitants, the medieval village was recently named by Forbes.com as one of the three most idyllic places in Europe to live.

A BOWL IN THE
process of being painted
and glazed at the *Ateliers
du Vieil Apt.* Faience, or
earthenware, has been
a specialty in this region
of France for centuries.

Each room in the multilevel house has a different *piece of art,* much of
it left by the *artists who have resided there.*

In the village of Saignon is a magical bed-and-breakfast called *Chambre avec Vue,* or "Room with a View," owned by Kamila Regent and Pierre Jaccaud. Parts of their home date back to the sixteenth century, however most of the art in it is very much of the twentieth and twenty-first centuries. Each room in the multilevel house has a piece of art, much of it left by the artists who have resided there. In addition to taking guests, Pierre and Kamila support artists who stay in their home for periods of time and share in communal meals. Generally the artists leave a work of art—either a painting, an installation, a photograph, or a manuscript of poetry. The couple started taking in artists in 1995 as part of a state-funded association in France called Mel or *Maison des Ecrivans et de la Litterature,* "The Institute of Writers and Literature," that promotes the arts.

The bed-and-breakfast has a large wooden door with a hand-shaped knocker that opens into a hallway with voluminous sheets of hand-painted fabrics strategically draped side-by-side and dancing in the breeze created from the opened door. Inside is a room with a video installation that has a loop of cutout papers with figures in silhouette that move on a track to recorded music from *The Magic Flute.* In the darkened room surrounded by stone walls from the Middle Ages, it creates a strange and unique experience.

FACING: In the Salon, tea is served using the fine earthenware of Apt. RIGHT: Flower detail on teacup.

Each floor displays art in the hallways as well as books and antiques. Upstairs in the salon is a grand piano, once owned by Andre Gide, one of the greatest French writers of the twentieth century.

Rooms are scattered haphazardly in the different levels of the house; moving through them is like walking through a maze or tumbling through a rabbit hole of installation art.

A wooden bridge suspended over the alleyway behind the house leads to a spacious garden, which is also a showplace for art. There, lunch was served in the garden under an enormous pear tree on a table that can seat twenty convivial guests.

The closest large town to Saignon is Apt, where faience or earthenware has been a specialty for several centuries. Fine faience from Apt appeared in the first half of the eighteenth century and it has been collected by many of the noble houses in France. Not far from Kamila and Pierre's bed-and-breakfast is the workshop called *Ateliers du Vieil Apt,* which was started by Luc Jacquel and Benoit Gils in 2003 after they worked at the atelier of Jean Faucon, a sixth-generation potter. *Ateliers du Vieil Apt* includes a small showroom on the street and then a slightly larger workshop in back in which Benoit and Luc painstakingly create their astonishing pottery by hand. Each piece is put together according to eighteenth-

ABOVE: Gooseberries, related to currants, are a fruit still uncommon in the United States today, though they were used in Colonial times. They have a unique taste and can be eaten fresh or cooked in various recipes such as pies, jams, and sauces. FACING: The table is set with faience from *Ateliers du Vieil Apt*.

century methods. The colors are natural dyes derived from the few remaining ochre mines in the region. Each flower adorning the dishes takes several hours to complete. The process is slow and detailed, from the molding to the firing to the glazing at the end. These are dishes that will be treasured for generations by the people who purchase them. It is amazing how much work goes into their products, as is the case with so many of the products of the small artisans in France.

Kamila arranged "Tea with Mama" in the downstairs salon. She sat in an eighteenth-century *chauffeuse* (a chair that is usually small and close to the fireplace so you can warm yourself) looking out to the cobblestoned street that goes past the entrance to the house. A selection of pastries and candies from Apt, which included *calissons d'aix,* the classic cookies from the region made with almond paste, were served, as well as gooseberries, pears, greengage plums, and a pear tart. All of this was displayed on the faience from Luc and Benoit's atelier.

Then in the garden, in the soft light of the Provencal sun, a table for a wine, cheese, and a fruit course was set, also featuring the faience from Apt. The table was under the large pear tree that would occasionally drop pears while we dined, a somewhat dangerous endeavor given the firmness of the pears!

In the garden, in the soft light of the
Provencal sun, a table for wine, cheese, and a fruit course
was set, also featuring the *faience from Apt.*

Several different breads were served with the *cheese* for these outdoor *evening hors d'oeuvres,* including a fougasse filled with olives, one of the specialties of Provence.

FOUGASSE WITH OLIVES

2¼ cups flour
1 rounded teaspoon yeast
½ teaspoon finely ground sea salt
4 tablespoons olive oil + more for brushing
¾ cup lukewarm water
½ cup pitted kalamata or Gaeta olives, cut in half

1   Put the flour, yeast, and salt in a bowl and mix. Add the olive oil in a stream to the flour mixture, and then add the lukewarm water and shape the dough into a ball. Knead the dough on a floured board for about 10 minutes. If it feels sticky add more flour.

2   Place the dough in the bowl and cover loosely with a towel. Leave in a warm place until it doubles in size (between 1 to 1½ hours). Punch the dough down and roll it out into an oval shape until it is about ½ inch thick.

3   Preheat the oven to 400 degrees F. Using a knife, cut an incision in the dough lengthwise. Then make slits (as if forming the branches of a tree) on each side of the incision. Stick the olive halves in the slits. Brush the fougasse with olive oil and place on a sheet pan that has also been brushed with oil. Bake for 20 minutes; remove from oven and place on a rack to cool.

Wine Pairing: Cotes de Luberon red

IN L'ISLE SUR LA SORGUE

In L'Isle Sur La Sorgue

Couscous Dinner

WHEN I MENTIONED to a French friend that I'd heard that couscous had been dubbed the new national dish of France by the venerable *Le Monde* newspaper, he visibly blanched. "What about *coq au vin, boeuf bourguignon, steak frites?*" he asked. I understood his consternation. France has changed quite a bit over the past thirty years since I lived there. With an influx of immigrants from many places, most notably North Africa, French cooking has changed a lot as well, and chefs are more open to such spices as cumin, cardamom, and turmeric. Lemon grass and ginger have become part of the culinary lexicon. While classic French cuisine certainly exists and is still passed from one generation to the next, it is undeniable that other cultures have made their mark at the restaurants and dinner tables of the country.

A VARIETY OF
HERBS are grown next
to the wall of the house.
The sculpture is by
Daniel Bonhomme.

The *stone walls* are varying shades of *blush pink* and *pale yellow*—colors found only in Provence or perhaps *Morocco*.

Eating couscous is now as common for the French as eating pizza is for Americans of all backgrounds in the United States. It is served at restaurants in small towns and in big cities. However, what most people order is the traditional couscous cooked with *merguez,* a spicy lamb sausage, chicken, and other meats. This is the couscous that was brought to France by the *Pieds-Noirs,* or people born in Algeria, who migrated to France after the Algerian war. This recipe is only one of many types of couscous recipes. Traditional couscous is really more comparable to pasta and is prepared in many different ways according to the season, the availability of ingredients, and the cook's personal tastes and background. And like pasta, couscous is not a grain—it is the product of the durum wheat kernel that is more coarsely ground than other flours. This is called semolina and it is used to make both pasta and couscous. There are some food historians who think couscous originated in the Sudan and then was adapted further north by the Berbers. The Berbers are often confused with Arabs; however they are not Arabs, but rather a distinct people with their own history in North Africa.

LEFT: A "green wall" covered in succulents and other plants is kept constantly moist by a simple yet sophisticated drainage system. It serves as a perfect backdrop for a sculpture by J-R Kokobi. RIGHT: Idyllic outdoor garden dining.

Ounouh is an Algerian-born artist who owns an art gallery called *Espace Libre* with his partner, Donald B. Ourligueux. The gallery is in the downstairs part of their home in the town of L'isle sur la Sorgue. On the outside it appears to be another attached townhouse that may or may not have been renovated. Inside it is a veritable wonderland of art from many periods and many countries.

Upstairs, the salon has formal furniture from nineteenth-century France intermingled with tribal sculptures, eighteenth-century porcelain vases, and paintings that look like they are from the Dutch masters. The stone walls of the interior are varying shades of blush pink and pale yellow—colors found only in Provence or perhaps Morocco.

In the gallery downstairs there is a green wall, a vertical installation of succulents and other plants that is constantly kept moist by a simple yet sophisticated drainage system. Another part of the interior courtyard has an herb garden surrounded by sculptures.

The table for lunch was set outside in the courtyard, under one of the chandeliers that Ounouh has crafted, which are much sought-after by decorators and art collectors. There was a vast selection of dishes to choose from, as Ounouh and Donald are connoisseurs of

ABOVE: A Picasso-like sculpture stands at the entrance to the outdoor dining area.

FACING: Tables and benches are handwrought from massive boughs of wood.

The *silverware*

is traditional French *sterling*.

PLATES ARE EDGED with a classical Greek motif. Notice the forks are placed tines down in the traditional style of French table setting.

many different styles and periods, and their pantry, as well as their décor, is a testament to their far-reaching tastes. It would have been simplest to use earthenware plates to serve the couscous, but we preferred to have a more elegant contrast to the handwrought wood table and therefore instead chose plates from the eighteenth-century with a Greek motif and handblown glasses from Venice. The silverware was traditional French sterling.

The couscous that Donald and Ounouh made was particularly suited to the heat of a midsummer evening. It was brought to the table in an Algerian bowl of rough earthenware and topped with zucchini flowers that were purchased at the market only an hour before. This last gesture made the meal seem as much French as Berber, a true melding of cultures inspired by the love of bringing people together through entertaining.

This is a recipe for a summer couscous made with vegetables— zucchini flowers are optional.

ALGERIAN COUSCOUS

2 tablespoons butter
1 large onion, minced
½ teaspoon turmeric
½ teaspoon cayenne pepper
4 whole cloves
1 teaspoon sea salt
1 cup vegetable stock
2 tablespoons tomato paste
2 red or orange peppers, sliced into
 ¼-inch slices

2 green zucchini (about ¾ pound),
 sliced into ½-inch slices
2 yellow zucchini (about ¾ pound),
 sliced into ½-inch slices
1 bunch fresh carrots, sliced
 diagonally into ½-inch slices
6 new potatoes, with skins on, halved
½ teaspoon cinnamon
1 can (15 ounces) chickpeas, drained
1 box fast-cooking couscous

1   Melt butter in a large stockpot over low heat. Add onion and sauté until it is soft, but not browned. Add turmeric, cayenne pepper, cloves, salt, and stock; let simmer for several minutes.

2   Stir in tomato paste. Then add the vegetables and enough water to cover completely. Turn up heat and bring the mixture to a boil, then cover the pot with a lid. Reduce heat and cook at a simmer for about 1 hour or until the vegetables are soft.

3   Add cinnamon and chickpeas and continue to cook the vegetables as you make the couscous. Drain 1 cup of liquid to use in making the couscous.

4   Make 1 box of couscous in a 2-quart pot according to the package directions, substituting the cup of vegetable stock for water. When couscous is finished, fluff it up and put it in a large serving bowl. Ladle the vegetables and their broth over the top and serve.

Wine Pairing: Cote de Provence Rose Domaine Ott

Tarte de Quetsches avec
flan

– 1 pâte feuilletée
– 700gr de quetsches
– 3 oeufs
– 1/2 l de lait
– 5 c.à.s. de sucre

Préchauffez votre four 180°.
Posez la pâte dans votre plat et
piquez-la avec une fourchette.
Mettez-y les quetsches
coupées en deux dessus.
Faites le flan oeufs, le
lait et le sucre-le s
votre
Cuis

The market, *Le Marché,*

is a vital part of life in many

French towns and villages, an integral part of

the historic heritage of France.

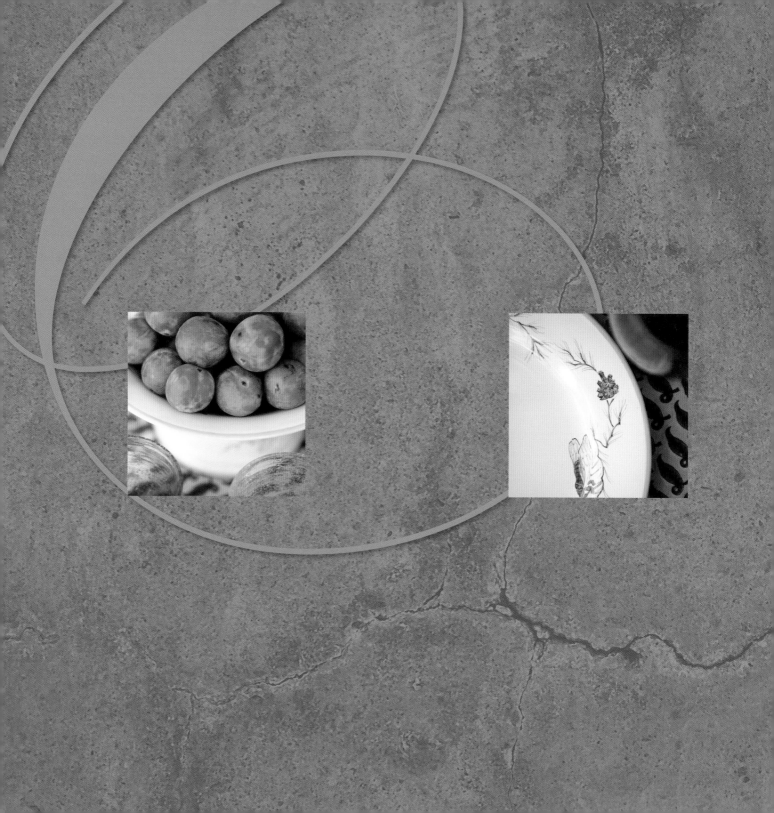

IN THE ANTIQUES CAPITAL OF FRANCE

In the Antiques Capital of France

Garden Lunch

L'ISLE SUR LA SORGUE is a city whose name means the island in the river Sorgue. It has been called the Venice of France after the many canals running through it. Like Venice, it was originally built on stilts in the water. There are numerous cafes and restaurants on the quays by the river, which make for a lively atmosphere, but the main attraction of L'isle sur la Sorgue is the antique stores. After Paris and London, it is considered to be the antiques center of Europe with more than three hundred shops in the small city. Twice a year, on the weekends of the fifteenth of August and on Easter, additional dealers also sell their wares, turning L'isle sur la Sorgue into a mecca for buyers of antiques. The Provence author, Peter Mayle, has been quoted as saying, "You can find many things in L'isle sur la Sorgue, but no bargains." And indeed, prices are often justifiably high.

ANTIQUE TEXTILES
from India decorate
the walls and furniture
and are for sale.

Michel Biehn has been a fixture of L'isle sur la Sorgue for almost two decades. He is a food writer, interior designer, and collector of antique furniture and textiles, particularly *Indiennes,* hand-blocked fabrics first brought to Provence from India by traders in the seventeenth century. These fabrics were once so popular that in 1686, the French government banned their import and manufacture because they felt it hurt the silk industry, which had been particularly important in Provence. Fortunately the ban was lifted in 1759 and the beautiful fabrics of Pierre Frey, Soleido, and others grace many homes in France and throughout the world.

In addition to collecting old textiles, Michel Biehn manufactures and designs *boutis* (quilted French fabric), which he has made for him in India. His collection of fabrics and dishes is sourced from his many travels to the East. He is a sorcerer of fabric and design, conjuring up magic in every corner of his shop.

Michel lives with his wife, Catherine, and family in an ivy-covered mansion from the nineteenth century. Enchantment reigns from every part of the home—from the vast

MOROCCAN POTTERY in blues and greens decorates the table and fresh goat cheese from a local farmers' market is adorned with a sprig of sage from Michel's garden.

garden backing the river Sorgue to the closets of hand-dyed fabrics and costumes to the stone walls covered with ivy. Their collection of dishes ranges from Moroccan pottery to floral-patterned dessert plates that were once in the possession of the actor David Niven.

The table that was set for the garden lunch was very much in Michel Biehn's style, with pattern on pattern: blue and green cotton plaid napkins over a green patterned *Indienne* tablecloth; faience from Moustiers designed by Michel; Moroccan pottery in blue, green, and white; Reine Claude plums in chartreuse; tea biscuits; country-style bread; and handblown Venetian glasses in shades of blue. For some reason, everything works! This is the end result of the skilled eye of a longtime collector.

When we added cheese to the table, Michel found a fig tree in the garden, cut two leaves off, and placed them under the cheese on the platter. The cheese was topped with some fresh sage that he also plucked from his garden.

The botanical porcelain dishes pictured at right were once in the possession of actor David Niven.

The dishes pictured at right were designed by Michel Biehn and fabricated in Mouspiers, France. The earthenware cicadas can be used as knife rests.

LEFT: A lush
ivy-covered wall is
quintessentially French.
FACING: The green
chandelier over the
garden table unifies all
the different elements
of the table setting.

I asked Michel if he could give me a plum tart recipe using the Reine Claude plums that we had just photographed. He looked at me in mock horror. "But you wouldn't use those plums for a tart, would you?" Reine Claude plums, also known as greengage plums, have an interesting history. Originally from Asia Minor, they were introduced in France sometime during the sixteenth century. They were named after Queen Claude, wife of Francis I of France, who died at the tender age of twenty-four. Later they were called greengage plums after Sir William Gage, an English botanist who brought them to England around 1725. Both Thomas Jefferson and George Washington cultivated these imported plums at their plantations. Greengage plums are sweet: perfect for jams and preserves; however, in Michel Biehn's opinion, not for use in tarts!

They do however make a perfect metaphor for a transitional table showing the influence of the East (India, China, Morocco) on the West and vice versa.

Here is a recipe for an easy-to-make *Plum Tart,*

called a *clafouti,* using purple plums.

PLUM CLAFOUTI

1 pound Italian blue plums,* pitted and
    cut in half
3 tablespoons sugar
Zest of 1 lemon
½ cup flour
Dash salt
2 eggs

3 tablespoons sugar
2 tablespoons sour cream or heavy cream
⅔ cup milk
Confectioner's sugar for serving

*Greengage plums may be substituted

1   Preheat oven to 375 degrees F. Place plums, skin side down, in a 10-inch tart pan.
    Sprinkle sugar and lemon zest over the top. Bake in preheated oven for 12 minutes;
    remove from oven.

2   In a medium bowl, whisk together flour, salt, and eggs until smooth. Mix in sugar,
    cream, and milk. Pour the mixture over the plums. Bake for 20 minutes, or until cus-
    tard is set and firm, and remove from oven. Sprinkle with confectioner's sugar and
    serve warm.

Wine Pairing: Baumes de Venise

In the Countryside Near Provence

IN THE COUNTRYSIDE NEAR PROVENCE

Three-Course Dinner

IT IS SAID THAT the French Resistance against the German occupation first started in the Alpilles, the mountain range south of Avignon that is officially a part of the Luberon Mountains. The Resistance fighters were called the *maquis* or *maquisards. Maquis* is loosely translated from the French as "scruff" or "brush" and when you go to the hills off the Alpilles, you can almost imagine the tough *maquisards* with their trademark berets hiding out in this lonely, desolate terrain.

While the towns are now filled with tourists during the warmer months, and quite a bit of the countryside is inhabited by people with second homes there, the mountains themselves can be isolating and severe. It is in this area that Tony Ramos lives with a panoramic view of the uninhabited land and mountains in the shadow of the ruins of a castle built in the twelfth century.

Tony is a multitalented painter and video artist of Cape Verdean descent who grew up in East Providence, Rhode Island. He exhibits his work in the United States and France and has made France his home for over a decade.

Approaching Tony Ramos's home near Eygalieres in Provence feels as if you are coming to the end of the world. The directions are simple: go to the first small town you see past the autoroute, drive over the railroad tracks, and watch for the vineyards on the right. Then when the vineyards stop, make a left turn onto a dirt road. Watch out for the chickens.

Ah, the ubiquitous chickens! It seems everyone in the countryside has chickens. They roam freely outside the homes and seem to fear little.

Tony lives and works in a farmhouse constructed of parts that date back to the twelfth century. His painting studio is a former stable with an ancient trough for the animals that lived there; the view through the open windows is not unlike the view that Van Gogh recreated in his master paintings of the Alpilles.

DINNER IS ROAST chicken from the market in Saint Remy de Provence and string beans with fresh tomatoes from the garden. It is served with red wine from the Alpilles region.

The home and studio are rustic and isolated, with no television and no computer to interfere with creative time. Entertaining is casual and artful, and Tony uses the magnificent views as a backdrop for the simple, locally prepared food.

Preparing dinner at his farmhouse began in the nearby market in Saint Remy de Provence on Wednesday morning. The town of Saint Remy de Provence has had a market on Wednesday mornings for centuries and it is filled to this day with artisans, farmers, locals, and tourists, particularly in summer. Artisanal saucisson, endless varieties of olives, and fruits and vegetables of the season are displayed at the market in individual booths manned by local producers and their families. The panoply of different wares makes it hard to concentrate, much less focus on, purchasing.

A three-part dinner is decided on, to take advantage of the sunset that in midsummer doesn't really start going down until after 9:00 p.m. First, hors d'oeuvres in the studio, then vin d'orange on the hill, and finally a leisurely buffet on the long artist's table where Tony does much of his work.

LEFT: The artist's tools, including pastels. FACING: Hors d'oeuvres are served before dinner along with the vin d'orange.

The working part of the studio is set up for hors d'oeuvres. On the wooden board covering the trough are sculptural vases made by Tony and hand-fired at a workshop in Aix en Provence called *Atelier Buffile* that specializes in traditional techniques for creating earthenware. The dishes used for the buffet were also made by Tony and finished at the same workshop. This is clearly the home of an artist who pays attention to detail and design in every aspect of his life. The sofa is covered in a large white banquet cloth that was found at the nearby market in Saint Remy de Provence—a reclaimed object. The same cloth is later used to cover the table holding the buffet.

The hors d'oeuvres included three different types of saucisson, all of them looking very rough and handmade; ten different kinds of olives; olive paste both green and black; and several types of bread.

Dinner featured the roast chicken purchased earlier from the market in Saint Remy de Provence, still warm from the waxed bag that it was packed in. String beans from the market were combined with fresh tomatoes from the garden. And local cheeses were laid out on the buffet table.

With the sun setting, we went off to

the hill behind the house to take in the view over the hills.

It was here that we tasted the vin d'orange, or

Orange Wine, a traditional

Provencal drink that has recently come back in fashion.

The taste of the cold *Sweet Wine*
under the setting sun overlooking the Alpilles mountains lingers as the
perfect memory of simple delights.

With the sun setting, we went off to the hill behind the house to take in the view over the hills. It was here that we tasted the *vin d'orange,* or orange wine, a traditional Provencal drink that has recently come back in fashion. Vin d'orange is not wine from the city of Orange in France; rather it is an infusion of bitter oranges (usually Seville or blood oranges), sugar, *eau de vie* (clear fruit brandy) and white wine, which is left to macerate for at least forty days. It is traditionally made in the month of March when oranges are at their best, and drunk as an apéritif or an after-dinner liquor in the summer. It is now commercially available in wine stores in France, but has always been best as a home brew, made by families and given to close friends and family members as a gift. The recipes are often found on handwritten paper passed from generation to generation. If you can allow it to brew for nine months without drinking it, vin d'orange makes a perfect Christmas gift.

The taste of the cold sweet wine under the setting sun overlooking the Alpilles mountains lingers as the perfect memory of the simple delights of this isolated farmhouse and the pleasures of sharing dinner with friends.

If you can allow it to brew for nine months

without drinking it, vin d'orange

makes a perfect Christmas gift.

VIN D'ORANGE

6 Seville oranges, washed,
  dried, and quartered
2 bottles white wine or rose wine
½ bottle eau de vie or vodka

2 cups sugar
Several whole cloves
1 vanilla bean

Mix all the ingredients in a large glass container and stir. Seal the container and store in a dark cool place (such as a cellar) for three to nine months, checking the mixture and stirring occasionally. Strain and put in sealed bottles. Serve cold.

In the Village of Maillane

Romantic French Breakfast

MAILLANE, A SMALL VILLAGE in the Alpilles near the market town of Saint Remy de Provence, was home to one of the greatest and most beloved French poets of the nineteenth and early twentieth centuries, Frederic Mistral. He won the Nobel Prize for Literature in 1904 and was responsible for the revival of the Old Provencal language and dialect during his lifetime. Mistral was born in Maillane and died there; the mansion he lived in is now a museum.

In Maillane, there are two bakeries, one grocery store, a pharmacy, and several restaurants and cafes, as well as a church, Saint Agathe. Life doesn't seem very different from the way that it

Our French breakfast in Maillane consists of
coffee, brioche, croissant, jam, pound cake, and melons.

probably was when Frederic Mistral lived there more than a hundred years ago. Mistral's poetry celebrated the land, the people, and the language itself. The museum devoted to him is a testament to the continuity, enduring land, and unchanging life of Provence.

Our French breakfast in Maillane consists of coffee, brioche, and croissant with lavender-flavored peach jam, freshly baked pound cake, white currants, and melon from Cavaillon, a nearby town in Provence whose sole industry is the production of these succulent melons. The Cavaillon melons were brought to France in the fourteenth century from Cantalupo, Italy, when the pope was installed in Avignon. Today, the melons are grown from seed and take almost three months to fully ripen and become ready to eat. There is definitely an art to choosing a melon—not picking it from the vine when it is either too ripe or too under-developed. The producers from Cavaillon have mastered this art and it is rare to purchase a melon that is not close to perfection. There is an official *melon de cavaillon* certification in France and a website: www.melondecavaillon.com devoted to these exceptional melons.

Morning coffee is enjoyed in a large-bowled traditional cup. Because the cup is so large—twice the size of an average American coffee cup—French coffee would become cold very quickly were it not for the heated milk always served with it.

Later in the day, after a romantic breakfast, a typical lunch in Maillane would include

IN THE BLUE BEDROOM, breakfast is served on Portuguese white earthenware. The melon, a cavaillon, was picked only yesterday and is fully ripe. The melon is not refrigerated, to keep its sun-ripened flavor.

LEFT: Famous white kidney beans, or flageolets, "the caviar of beans," make a great salad in the summer and a delicious soup in the winter. FACING: Produce and herbs make a splendid centerpiece for the table.

vegetables such as the ones artfully arranged in a pyramid in the center of the dining table: tomatoes, artichokes, garlic, and onions flanked by several varieties of dried beans and herbs. The bread is rough and country-like, served with local cheese (purchased from the farmer on the road to Saint Remy de Provence), and topped with a cherry confiture. These pairings have become increasingly popular in France as well as in the United States; they are similar to the pairings of cheese and honey in such other Mediterranean areas as Sicily, Corsica, Turkey, and Greece. The cherry confiture is an excellent condiment for cheese or goes well served with toast or croissants for breakfast.

For dessert, what could be better than locally grown

Raspberries with créme fraîche and a promenade to

Saint Remy de Provence down the royal way?

Cherry confiture is an excellent condiment for Cheese or goes well served with Toast or Croissants for breakfast.

CHERRY CONFITURE

3 cups cherries
Juice of 1 lemon
2 cups sugar

1   Pit the cherries and cut them into pieces. Place them in a thick, nonreactive, deep saucepan with the lemon juice and cook over low heat until cherries are soft and glistening, about 15 minutes. Stir using a wooden spoon; make sure that they cook evenly and do not burn.

2   Add sugar and continue to stir over low heat until the sugar is dissolved. Once the fruit mixture is no longer granular, raise the heat and cook until it coats the back of the wooden spoon, about 10 minutes. Be careful not to burn the cherries. If you use a candy thermometer, the temperature will reach 220 degrees F and the cherries will be done. The jam will become gluey if it is overcooked.

3   Pour the cherry confiture into sterilized canning jars, cover, and refrigerate.

Wine Pairing: Bandol red

ARBRES D'ALIGNEMENT,
or plane trees, lining
the road are seen
throughout France.
This is the road from
Maillane to Saint
Remy de Provence.

In the Heart
of Burgundy

Cooking with Flowers

ALICE CARON LAMBERT is a poet and writer who has written more than a thousand recipes using flowers in her fourteen published cookbooks. One could say that she is the Johnny Appleseed of cooking with edible flowers. She distinguishes the tastes between hundreds of different varieties of roses and chrysanthemums and shows how to cook salmon with rose flavoring, begonia soup, lentils with daffodils, and broccoli with mimosa, among many other recipes.

Alice lives in Burgundy in a splendid farmhouse with sections that date back to the fifteenth century. The stone walls in the fifteenth-century section feature chiseled-out hearts in homage to Jacques Coeur, the heart being a symbol of his last name, *coeur* or *heart.* Coeur, born at the end of the Hundred Years War, had

"A Vaillant Coeur, rien impossible"
"For a valiant heart, nothing is impossible"

MOTTO OF JACQUES COEUR C 1395–1456
MINISTER OF FINANCE UNDER CHARLES VII

a swashbuckling history. He was the son of a trader in Bourges, a city in central France, and rose to become the treasurer of the mint and one of the wealthiest Frenchmen of his time due to his business dealings with Charles VII. At the time of Jacques Coeur, the seat of the French government had been established at Bourges. Coeur financed wars for Charles VII and established trade with several countries in the Middle East, making for himself a vast fortune. He lent many in the court money, which possibly ultimately led to his downfall. He was jailed for poisoning the king's mistress soon after he achieved his greatest prominence. It was said that he was set up by jealous courtiers who owed him money. After three years in prison, Coeur (probably with official help) escaped and went to Rome. He ended up in Chios, Greece, where he died manning a crusade for the pope against the Ottomans. He had homes all over France, one of them a magnificent palace in Bourges, which exists as a museum today. Although it is not certain, the home in Dracy where Alice lives might have been one of his residences.

Alice's home has hearts carved in the stone walls and beautiful flowers growing around the various parts of the house.

A JASMINE TART
flavored with violet
extract is garnished with
crystallized mint leaves
and rose petals from
the organic garden.

For our visit, Alice made a jasmine tart with raisins flavored with violet extract and decorated with crystallized rose petals and mint leaves. The crystallized mint tasted like the es-
sence of mint with a freshness that bristled on the tongue. She also made a pound cake, or
quatre quarts, flavored with rose water. The reason a true French pound cake is called a *quatre
quarts,* or literally "four-fourths," is that it originally consisted of four equal parts by weight:
one pound of eggs, one pound of flour, one pound of butter, and one pound of sugar. It is
a classically deceptive recipe of only four ingredients, all of which are equally important.
Traditionally there is no baking powder in a French pound cake. The leavening is achieved
by creaming the butter and whipping the egg whites.

In addition to her many cookbooks and lectures on cooking with flowers, Alice is a
member of the World Wide Organisation of Organic Farming, or www.wwoof.org, which
encourages home stays by people on working farms. Alice had three students staying with
her—one from Israel, one from Ireland, and one from Normandy. They were all there to
learn from the culture of an organic working farm. Everything on the farm is organic, from
the eggs laid by the chickens roaming freely on the property to the roses and herbs growing
in the garden.

THIS PAGE: Alice clipping roses from her organic rose garden; the scent of the fresh roses is subtle and sublime. FACING: The table is set to enjoy a late afternoon tea. Outside, the sun shines through the window of the splendid Burgundy farmhouse with parts that date back to the fifteenth century. A rhubarb and raisin tart flavored with jasmine syrup is served, and scents from the garden and the table create the ambiance of a floral heaven.

FACING: Kerry, an architecture student from Ireland, poses with a glass of fresh juice and a plate of crystallized rose petals and mint leaves.

The student from Israel explained that it was his first trip to France, and he was enthralled by the markets and the area, especially by the moat that surrounded the castle abutting Alice's property. A practicing vegetarian, he found it quite easy to have delicious and varied meals at the homes of people that he visited. The ease of practicing a vegetarian lifestyle shows a different France than it was thirty years ago when meals almost always were centered around a main course of meat or fish.

The table was set with the simplest dishes of white earthenware in the sun-filled dining area in order to highlight the colors of the roses, the mint leaves, and the jasmine-flavored tart. The table was decorated with fresh flowers Alice cut from her garden. A neighbor passing by paused to look at the setup as Kerry, another of the students, sat in the window gazing at the desserts in front of her and said, "That is a photograph worthy of a painting by Vermeer." And the setting was like a Vermeer, poetic in its celebration of domesticity and place. It was a magical moment when all of the lushness of Burgundy could be felt inside the afternoon light of the window. Truly as Jacques Coeur's motto says, "to the valiant of heart, nothing is impossible."

ANTIQUE DESSERT FORKS
with mother-of-pearl handles
add a sophisticated touch to
the country table setting.

For our visit, Alice made a *Jasmine tart*

with raisins flavored by violet extract and decorated

with crystallized rose petals and mint leaves.

There are many ways to make a traditional *French pound cake* or *quatre quarts*, but this is a favorite.

POUND CAKE OR QUATRE QUARTS

1 cup unsalted butter, softened
1 cup sugar
4 eggs, separated
Pinch salt
1 teaspoon vanilla extract or rose flower water
2 cups flour

1   Preheat oven to 375 degrees F. Butter a 10 x 5-inch loaf pan and set aside. In a medium bowl, cream the butter and beat in the sugar. Add egg yolks and beat until fluffy.

2   In a separate bowl, beat the egg whites with salt until stiff. Add vanilla or rose flower water. Stir flour into the creamed mixture, then carefully fold in the egg whites. Pour the batter into the prepared pan and bake for 40 minutes.

3   Remove from oven and cool on a cake rack before removing pound cake from pan.

Wine Pairings: Joseph Drouhin St. Veran 2008
                     Chardonnay

LEFT: The oldest part of the farmhouse is cool and protected from the heat of the summer with stone walls. ABOVE, RIGHT: The gorgeous church in the small town of Dracy. BELOW, RIGHT: The heart carving inset in stone is the symbol of Jacques Coeur.

IN LA PERCHE

In La Perche
Dinner and Calvados

WHEN READING ABOUT THE AREA of La Perche in France one often hears the French expression *terroir*. *Terroir* can be defined variously as soil or the land, and it is constantly used in relationship to wine, but the word means so much more than that. Terroir is the relationship of food to the land and the people who cultivate the land. It is the animals that graze upon the land, the agriculture, and the integrity of the food grown specific to the area. It is the angle of the sun, the accumulation of the rain, and the geographical location that makes up terroir. UNESCO's definition of the term is, in part, as follows:

"Terroirs" are vibrant and innovative spaces that define the people who live there and reflect a marriage between traditions, culture, and the natural environment."

LAITERIE
DE LA
FERME

La Perche, hidden in plain sight, is a region about one hundred miles west of Paris that few people, even Parisians, seem to know about. It has never achieved official department status in France; however, it is not particularly insignificant in size, being approximately as large as the state of Rhode Island. La Perche has been described as lower Normandy, yet it is a place that is far removed from the chic resorts of Deauville and Honfleur, which many call the twenty-first *arrondisements* of Paris for all the Parisians who have weekend homes there. La Perche is still predominantly agricultural; in fact, to be so close to a major city and still be so rooted in the land or *terroir* is its most significant and endearing feature.

The kitchen is the center or soul of the house.
The farmhouse table serves as a *gathering place* for friends.

A hand-painted sign on the way into La Perche announced artisanal cheese for sale. A farm called *La Chevroliere* produced raw milk cheese, cream, butter, and yogurt as well as fruit juice—all organic. The farm was designated *agriculture biologique,* or certified organic farm, because they use methods that respect nature—a concept that has been around for centuries, but has only been given official status in the past couple of decades.

Monique Duveau, a food writer and editor for such esteemed publications as *Cote Sud, Cote Ouest,* and *Elle Décor,* and her companion, Jose Esteves, a sculptor and lighting designer, came to the area three years ago to visit friends and were immediately taken with it. Their existence became completely rooted in *terroir.*

Monique and Jose bought an old girls' school called Ecole St Martin and transformed it into a very personal and warm country home that still retains vestiges of its pedagogical past. There is a theater on the grounds in which they have held parties, using the old props and dressing up in the costumes that the school left behind.

The formerly institutional kitchen is the center or soul of the house. They have made it relevant and functional with an old iron sink purchased from a florist, old wooden cabinets, and a large farmhouse table that serves as a gathering place for friends.

COUNTERCLOCK-WISE FROM TOP LEFT: Olive oil poured on vegetables for the pork; silver forks on a wooden table combines the rustic with the elegant; antique French saltcellars; cheese knives. FACING: The dining room offers a view to the potager, or French kitchen garden. These gardens can be simple plantings or elaborately landscaped such as the one created for Louis XIV at Versailles in the seventeenth century called the *potager du roi* or the king's garden. The chandelier over the dining table is Jose Estevez's creation.

LEFT: Local pear cider from Normandy.
FACING: Jose pours oil on the pork as it turns on the rotisserie. The rotisserie was handmade just outside of Paris and is the heart of the kitchen.

The heart of the kitchen is a La Cornue rotisserie, in a design that looks as if it dates back to medieval times even though it was made in the twenty-first century. The rotisserie was handmade just outside Paris in *La Cornue's Saint Ouen l'Aumône* atelier. It is the masterpiece of Xavier Dupuy, President of La Cornue and grandson of its 1908 founder, Albert Dupuy. Synthetic wicks pull the heat up through the vaulted back of the rotisserie, allowing the radiant heat to gently cook meat, poultry, or fish as it rotates slowly over the flame.

Monique has collections of old calvados glasses for *Le trou normande,* or the Norman Hole, and employs the tradition of a palate-cleansing break in the middle of dinner for a bracing shot of calvados. Great calvados from Normandy is a blend of more than one hundred different varieties of apples distilled into a liquor. The *trou normande* these days is often an iced sorbet that is served at multicourse dinners, rather than the little shot of dynamite that it used to be.

A COLLECTION OF old calvados glasses. These glasses are perfect for the tradition of a palate-cleansing break—*Le trou normande*—in the middle of dinner for a bracing shot of calvados.

Monique has tablecloths and napkins dyed using vegetable dyes, old
silverware, and an armoire filled with
earthenware known as *cul noir* that is
particular to Normandy and Brittany.
The table is set with plates of *cul noir*
colored in deep brown enamel that
seems as natural as the earth.

Above the farmhouse table in the
kitchen is one of Jose Esteves chandeliers. Many of his lighting fixtures
use recycled objects such as old silver
spoons and forks or other found ma-
terials. This philosophy reflects the
theme of *terroir* "a marriage between
traditions, culture, and the natural environment" that is emblematic of the
life that Jose and Monique have created in La Perche.

Dinner consisted of a roast pork, or *Roti de Porc,* made in the rotisserie.

ROAST LOIN OF PORK WITH POTATOES AND APPLES

ROAST

4 tablespoons olive oil

1 boneless pork roast, weighing approximately
  4 pounds, tied with string

4 cloves garlic, unpeeled

2 sprigs rosemary

Sea salt to taste

10 small red potatoes, parboiled with skins on

6 Cortland apples, cored, peeled, and cut in quarters

1 pound baby carrots

SAUCE

¼ cup calvados or apple cider

1 teaspoon coarsely ground peppercorns

2 teaspoons Dijon mustard

¾ cup heavy cream

1 Preheat oven to 325 degrees F. Use a large roasting pan with a cover that can go in the oven as well as on top of the stove. Heat 2 tablespoons of olive oil in the pan over medium heat, then add the pork and brown it on all sides. Add the garlic and rosemary. Salt liberally, cover, and place in the oven.

2 Let the roast cook for about 1 hour, then add the potatoes. After another ½ hour, add the apples and carrots. Cook until finished, about another ½ hour. A good measure is about 30 minutes per pound of meat.

3 Remove the pork from the oven and place it on a serving plate with the potatoes, carrots, and apples alongside. There should be quite a bit of juice from the pork in the pan. Pour the juice into a container and let the fat on top separate. Skim the fat off with a spoon.

4 Mash the softened garlic in the pan and remove the skin. Add the calvados or cider to the pan and stir with a wooden spoon until it reduces slightly. Swirl any browned bits from the pork in the pan with the sauce. Add the reserved juice to the pan and cook for several minutes at a high temperature. Add the peppercorns, mustard, and then the cream, all the while stirring with a wooden spoon until the cream thickens. Serve pork and vegetables with the cream on the side.

Wine Pairings: Loire Valley Red
        Clos de la Briderie Touraine-Mesland Rouge Vieilles Vigres 2007

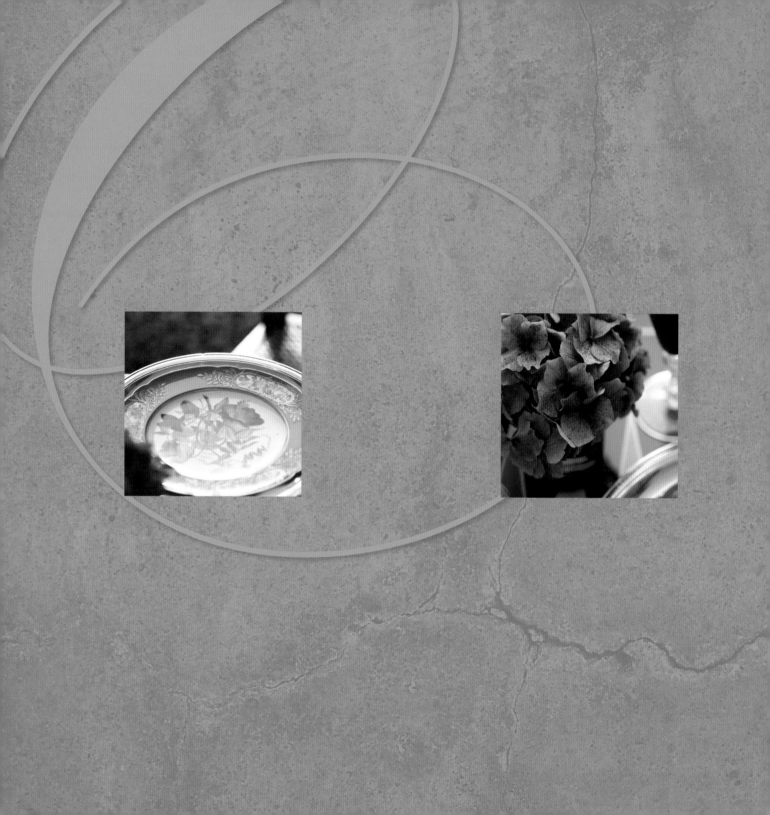

IN A PARIS APARTMENT

IN A PARIS APARTMENT
Quintessential City Dining

JEAN-PAUL BEAUJARD, a decorator who lives and works in New York and Paris, has created an apartment made for entertaining in his Left Bank duplex. For him, it is all about ambiance when he decorates a home. His living room with its high ceilings and tall French windows is airy and spacious—almost loft-like. Jean-Paul's home exudes a sense of place and that place is most definitely Paris.

A table is set in his living room for a chic lunch for six close friends. It is a quiet Sunday in Paris in late summer. Everyone is out of town for the August holiday and the city is quiet, almost pristine in its silence. Soon there will be noise on the streets, traffic that is almost unbearable, crowded restaurants, movie theaters with lines of people waiting to get in. But for one glorious month in summer, all is tranquil, and for the person who decides to stay in the city, there are many rewards.

Even in August,

the flower shops that remain open manage to dazzle. We were

lucky to find the shop Rosa Luna nearby the apartment.

In the apartment, the light flowing through the windows that are swathed in silk is expansive. The table is set with a china that is bordered with ivy and a cream-colored tablecloth of fine linen from Porthault, which has been making luxury table and bed linens in France for more than ninety years. The only decorations on the table are the two large candelabras at each end and several garlands of ivy forming a design that looks like a Roman Emperor's crest.

Even in August, the flower shops in Paris manage to dazzle, those that remain open at least. We were lucky to find Rosa Luna nearby the apartment, an enchanting shop of less than 400 square feet that reeks of Paris chic. We purchased the ivy and a giant hydrangea.

For hors d'oeuvres, the game table is set up in the library. This table was made by Maison Jansen, a decorating and manufacturing firm started by a Dutchman, Jean-Henri Jansen, in 1880. During the twentieth century, Maison Jansen supplied furniture to royal houses like the Shah of Iran, the Rothschilds, and the private rooms of the Kennedy White House. Their art objects and period furniture reproductions are greatly treasured today for their

meticulous manufacture and attention to detail. Even with the mix of styles and periods in the room, there is a sense of discipline as if everything has a place and a function.

The floral dishes are French soft-paste porcelain from Sevres, dating back to the eighteenth century. The glassware and the decanter are also eighteenth century. The hors d'oeuvres of blinis and fresh caviar are served.

TRADITIONAL BLINI AND CAVIAR

¼ cup lukewarm water
1 package active yeast
1½ teaspoons sugar
½ cup all-purpose flour
½ cup buckwheat flour
¼ teaspoon salt

1 cup milk, heated to lukewarm
¼ cup butter, melted, divided
2 large eggs
Melted butter for serving
3 ounces caviar
2 tablespoons sour cream

1   Stir together warm water, yeast, and sugar in a bowl and let stand until foamy, about 5 minutes. Add flours and salt, then stir in milk, 3 tablespoons of the melted butter, and eggs. Cover bowl with plastic wrap. Let rise in a warm place until batter is increased in volume and has bubbles breaking the surface, about 1½ to 2 hours. Stir batter before using.

2   Heat a 12-inch nonstick skillet over moderately high heat until hot and brush with some of the remaining melted butter. (If butter browns immediately, lower heat.) Working in batches of 4, spoon 1 tablespoon of batter into skillet for each blini, then cook, about 2 minutes, turning over once until golden on both sides. Transfer to an ovenproof platter and keep in a warm oven until ready to serve.

3   Serve each blini topped with melted butter, caviar, and a dollop of sour cream.

Wine Pairing: Champagne

LEFT: The floral dishes are French soft-paste porcelain from Sevres, dating back to the eighteenth century.
FACING: The decanter is a late eighteenth-century design.

LEFT: Detail of the
candelabra's frond design.
FACING: In Paris in summer,
the sun is still shining until
9:00 or 9:30 p.m., so
Parisians often enjoy late
evening dinners before dusk
falls. The sun filters into
the apartment showing the
ivy-themed table setting
to great advantage.

Art objects are greatly treasured by the French for their
meticulous manufacture and *attention to detail.*

Resources

Alice Caron Lambert

www.floralice.com

*Gives recipes using
flowers as ingredients*

**The AOC rating (Appellation
d'origine controlee)**

*Institute that regulates agricultural
products in France (including wines
and cheeses) giving the AOC rating*

**Institute National de
l'Origine et de la Qualite**

www.inao.gouv.fr/

Jean-Paul Beaujard

jpbeaujardinc@gmail.com

Decorator

Michel Biehn

Le Jardin des Biehn

13, Akbat Sbaa, Douh

30200 - FEZ Medina

www.lejardindesbiehn.com

tel : 00 212 (0) 535 638 690

Food

The French Farm

www.frenchfarm.com

Cheese

www.cheesesoffrance.com

Information about French Cheese

Melissa's Produce

www.melissas.com

*A distributor for difficult-to-
find fruits and vegetables
such as gooseberries*

Melons from Cavaillon

www.melondecavaillon.com

Furnishings

Espace libre

51, Rue Carnot

84800 L'isle sur La Sorgue

ounouh@gmail.com

http://ounouh.jimdo.com/

*Chandeliers made by Ounough
in L'isle Sur la Sorgue*

Interieurs Showroom

Exclusively in the United States

228 East 58th Street

New York, NY 10022

www.interieurs.com

*Chandeliers made by Jose
Estevez in La Perche*

Tolix Chairs

www.tolix.fr/en

Galleries and Foundations for the Arts

Fondation Blachere

384 Avenue des Argiles

84400 Apt, France

www.fondationblachere.org

*A foundation in Apt that
specializes in contemporary
African Art. Pierre Jaccaud of
Saignon is the artistic director.*

Musée Baccarat

11 place des Etats Unis

75116 Paris

www.baccarat.com

Gallery-Museum

Tableware

Bernadäud New York

499 Park Avenue

New York, NY 10022

*Purveyors of French crystal,
porcelain, silverware*

Home, James!
55 Maine Street
East Hampton, NY 11037

4514 Travis Walk
Dallas, TX 75205
www.homejameseasthampton.com

In Paris
27 rue de Varenne,
Diners en Ville
*Sells new and antique tableware,
accessories, and luxury cloths*

L'Atelier
www.atelierduvieilapt.com
Earthenware pictured in Saignon

Museum of Sevres Porcelain
www.musee-ceramique-sevres.fr

WINES

Rosenthal Wine Merchant
1219 Route 83
Pine Plains, NY 12567
800-910-1990
518-398-5974 (fax)
www.madrose.com
*Importer of wines from
regional areas of France*

LODGINGS

**Bed and Breakfast for
Artists in Saignon, France**
www.chambreavecvue.com

Bambou in Maillane, France
www.bambouprovence.com
House for rent